The Abraham Lincoln Joke Book

by Beatrice Schenk de Regniers

Illustrations by
William Lahey Cummings

SCHOLASTIC INC.
New York Toronto London Auckland Sydney

Special Arrow Edition

ISBN 0-590-30968-4

12 11 10 9 8 7 6   9/8 0 1/9

Printed in the U.S.A.   08

*This book is dedicated to
everyone who loves Lincoln
and especially to boys and girls
in my home state, Indiana,
where Abraham Lincoln grew up*

School Days

Abraham Lincoln wrote that he "went to A.B.C. schools by littles"—a few weeks or a few months at a time. And all his schooling added together "did not amount to one year."

The rest of Lincoln's education came from reading, reading, reading—and from listening and from seeing and thinking about what was going on around him.

This is from one of Abraham Lincoln's school notebooks. He may have been about eleven years old when he wrote this:

Abraham Lincoln
his hand and pen .
he will be good but
god knows When

A Good Speller and
a Good Friend

Abe Lincoln was eleven years old when he went
to Andrew Crawford's school in Indiana. Schoolmaster Crawford taught reading, writing, spell-
ing, arithmetic, and manners.

Kate Roby went to Crawford's school with
Abe Lincoln. Years later she told what happened one day. Her story shows that Abe was
a good speller—and a good friend.

It was Kate Roby's turn to spell the word *defied*—as in "The brave lad *defied* the giant."

Three children had already spelled the word wrong. Schoolmaster Crawford was getting angry.

"D-e-f," Kate began. Then she stopped. Was the next letter *i* or *y*? She looked across the room.

There was Abe Lincoln, grinning at her— and he was pointing to his eye.

Kate took the hint and spelled the word with an *i*. That was one word she never forgot how to spell.

Captain Lincoln

Chief Black Hawk was on the war path. Long ago his tribe had sold their land in Illinois to the United States. Now Chief Black Hawk said, "Land cannot be sold. The land still belongs to us."

He was coming with 500 Indian warriors to get his land back—and to kill any palefaces who tried to stop him.

The United States government sent soldiers from the regular army to fight the Indians. Lincoln and his friends in Illinois joined the army. They were volunteers and could choose their own captain. They chose Lincoln.

Lincoln was only 23 years old. He was pleased and proud that the men wanted him for their captain. But Lincoln didn't know much

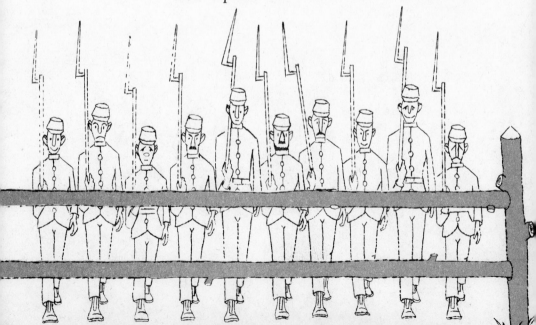

about soldiering. Later he liked to tell about the time he was drilling his men:

Lincoln had twenty men marching side by side across a field.

They came to a fence and had to pass through a narrow gate to get to the next field. It was up to Captain Lincoln to give the right command so that the men could line up behind one another, two by two, and get through the gate.

"But," said Lincoln, "I could not for the life of me remember the proper word of command to get my company endwise so that it could go through the gate. So, as we came near the gate, I shouted:

" 'This Company is dismissed for two minutes, when it will fall in again on the other side of the gate.' "

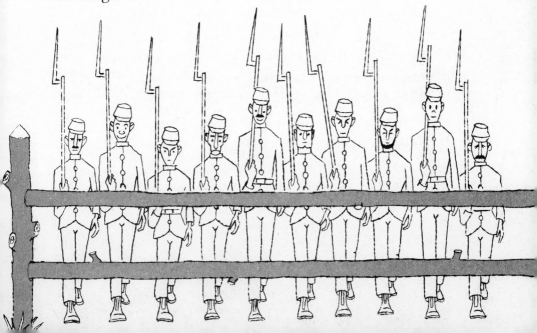

A Joe Miller Pun

This pun is from Joe Miller's joke book, Lincoln's favorite book of funny stories.

Q: What was the name of Black Hawk's son?

A: Tommy Hawk (tomahawk), of course.

The Wrong (?) Place

When Lincoln was a traveling lawyer, he would stay with other lawyers at the one tavern, or hotel, in town.

At mealtime, everyone sat at one long table. Lawyers, judges, jurymen, witnesses, prisoners, peddlers—everyone who had business at the court or in the town sat at the same table. But the landlord always had the judges and lawyers sit together at the head of the table.

One day Lincoln came in and sat at the foot of the table with the prisoners and peddlers.

"Mr. Lincoln!" the landlord called. "You're in the wrong place. Come up here."

"Have you anything better to eat up there, Joe?" asked Lincoln with a smile. "If not, I'll stay here."

Horse Trade

For years people in Illinois laughed about the horse trade between lawyer Lincoln and a judge:

Lincoln and the judge were joking about who could make the better horse trade. At last they agreed to meet in the morning to swap horses. Lincoln would not see the judge's horse beforehand. And the judge would not see Lincoln's horse.

The next morning a crowd gathered. Who would get the better of the trade?

The judge came first, dragging behind him the oldest, sorriest, boniest nag that ever managed to stand on four feet.

While the crowd was still laughing, Lincoln came along, carrying a carpenter's wooden saw horse. For a full minute Lincoln stared at the judge's horse without saying a word.

"Judge," said Lincoln at last, "this is the first time I ever got the worst of it in a horse trade."

No Trouble

Lawyer Lincoln, so they say, was walking along a dusty road. Along came a farmer driving his wagon to town.

LINCOLN: Would you be good enough to take my overcoat to town for me?

FARMER: Glad to. But how will you get it back again?

LINCOLN: No trouble at all. I'm going to stay right inside it!

The Mysterious Visitor

When Lincoln was a traveling lawyer, he arranged to have a young man named Smith stay with Mrs. Lincoln and the two children at their home in Springfield.

About two o'clock one dark morning when Lincoln was away, Smith was wakened by Mrs. Lincoln.

There were queer noises at the pantry window, Mrs. Lincoln said. Someone was trying to get into the house!

Could it be an enemy of Lincoln's? A burglar?

Smith could hear someone working away at the shutters of the pantry window. *Rattle, rattle, rattle.*

How could he get help quickly? There were no phones then. He would have to go to the nearest house, which was some distance away.

Smith opened the front door quietly and slipped out. Now the noise at the shutters sounded louder than ever. Smith peered around the corner of the house—and burst out laughing.

As Smith himself told the story later, "Something sweet had been spilled out of the pantry window that day, and a Jersey cow was enjoying it." The cow was running her tongue up and down the shutters to lick the sweet stuff. And that was what made the mysterious rattling noise!

Lincoln came home later that morning, laughed when he heard what had happened, and for years afterward enjoyed telling the story to friends.

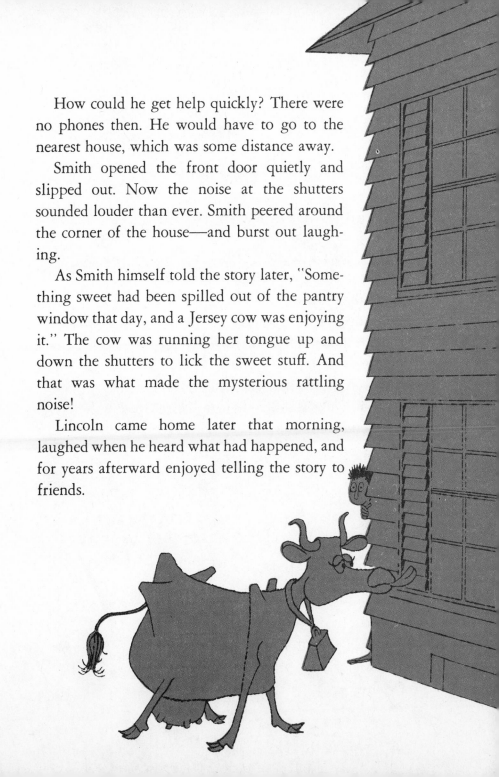

Turn Out!

Another story was told about Lincoln when he was a lawyer.

This time, Lincoln was driving a wagon along a muddy road when he met a man driving in the other direction. The road was narrow. One of the men would have to "turn out." That is, he would have to turn his horse to the right and get off the road—and into the ditch.

But the ditch was muddy And the man who turned out was likely to get stuck in the mud.

"Turn out!" called the man.

"Turn out yourself," said Lincoln.

"I won't!" the man shouted.

Lincoln began to stand up in his wagon. "If you don't turn out," said Lincoln—and he

looked taller and taller as he straightened up—
"I'll tell you what I'll do!"

The other man looked up at Lincoln. Lincoln seemed to be stretching higher and higher against the sky.

"Stop!" shouted the man. "Don't go any higher. I'll turn out!"

The man turned out and finally managed to get his wagon past Lincoln's. But before going on, he stopped and shouted back, "Now what would you have done if I hadn't turned out?"

Said Lincoln, "I'd have turned out myself."

Everyone Happy

When Lincoln was a lawyer, he tried to make peace between men. That was more important to him than making money.

Once he had to play a joke on someone in order to make peace. This is what happened:

A rich man who had just moved to Springfield wanted to sue a poor man who owed him two dollars and fifty cents. And the rich man wanted Lincoln to be his lawyer.

Lincoln tried to talk the rich man out of suing the poor man.

"If you won't do the job for me," said the man, "I'll go to another lawyer."

So Lincoln said he would take the case. "But you must pay my fee now," said Lincoln. "Ten dollars."

The rich man paid Lincoln the ten dollars.

Then Lincoln went to the poor man who owed the money. Lincoln gave the man five dollars and told him to come to court the next day and pay the money he owed.

The poor man came, paid the two dollars and fifty cents to the rich man, and everyone was happy:

The rich man had his revenge—he thought.
The poor man got some extra money.

Lincoln had five dollars left in payment for his trouble and time.

Ruffle-shirt Taylor

Sometimes actions speak louder than words— and are funnier than words, too.

When Lincoln was twenty-seven years old, he belonged to a political party called Whigs. Lincoln was running for the Illinois State legislature against Dick Taylor.

Taylor was good-looking and stuck-up. He liked to wear fancy clothes and was called "ruffle-shirt Taylor." But he knew he could get more votes if people thought he was a poor, hard-working man.

So when Taylor went on speaking trips to get votes, he would keep his coat buttoned up to hide his fine ruffled shirt. What was more, he talked about what a poor, hard-working man he was. And he said that Lincoln and all the other Whigs were rich aristocrats who wouldn't do a thing for the people.

One evening Dick Taylor and Abraham Lincoln were debating in front of a crowd of farmers. Taylor began talking again about what a poor, hard-working man he was.

Lincoln knew this was not true, and finally he decided to teach Taylor a lesson. While Taylor was talking, Lincoln slipped over to him and tore open Taylor's coat.

The surprised farmers got a fine view of Taylor's ruffled shirt, gorgeous velvet vest, and fancy watch chain ornamented with golden seals set with precious stones.

Then Lincoln gave *his* talk, and the farmers had a chance to listen to a man who really knew what it meant to be poor and to work hard.

P.S. Lincoln was elected.

According to the joke books Lincoln was the man who said:

"Waiter, if this is coffee, then please bring me some tea. But if this is tea, please bring me some coffee."

Lincoln once said of another lawyer who talked a lot and never said anything worth saying:

"That man can pack the *most words* into the *least ideas* of any man I know."

Hey! Hay!

Any good joke seemed better if it was called a Lincoln joke. Maybe that is why this joke was told as though it happened to Lincoln:

Lincoln was riding horseback on a country road, and found his way blocked by a big load of hay. The hay had fallen off a wagon. The boy driving the wagon was upset and excited.

"Now don't worry," Lincoln told the boy. "Come with me to the farmhouse and we'll find someone to help us get the hay back on the wagon.

At the farmhouse, the kindly farmer invited Lincoln and the boy to have dinner. Lincoln enjoyed his dinner, but he saw that the boy was worried and restless.

"Pa won't like this," the boy muttered. "Pa won't like this at all."

"Now don't you worry," Lincoln told the boy. "Your Pa knows that an accident can happen to anybody. No need to hurry." And Lincoln took a second helping of potatoes.

"Pa won't like my being away so long."

"Oh come now," said Lincoln. "Your Pa will understand. He would want you to take time out to eat a good dinner. I'll go with you and explain what happened. By the way, where is your Pa?"

"He's under the load of hay!" wailed the boy.

How Many d's?

Lincoln married pretty Mary Todd of Kentucky. Mary Todd's father was president of a bank and Mary had a good education, fine manners, fancy clothes. Some people thought the Todd family was stuck-up. Maybe that is why they made up this story:

"Why does the Todd family spell its name with two d's?" someone asked Lincoln. And he quickly replied, "I guess one 'd' is enough for God, but the Todds need two!"

Don't You Think You Can Stand It?

There were many stories about Mrs. Lincoln's quick temper and sharp tongue.

Here is one story that was told in Springfield, Illinois, where the Lincolns were living:

Lincoln's wife saw a delivery man spit on her clean back doorstep. Mrs. Lincoln lost her temper. Screaming loud enough for the whole neighborhood to hear, she told the man just what she thought of him.

The man was angry and insulted and he complained to Mr. Lincoln, who was standing on the front doorstep.

Lincoln said he was sorry and apologized for his wife's behavior. But the delivery man was still hopping mad.

Finally, Lincoln said, "My dear sir, if I have had to stand this every day for fifteen years, don't you think you can stand it a few minutes just one day?"

A neighbor met Lincoln walking along the street one sunny spring morning.

LINCOLN: It's a great day for the race.

NEIGHBOR: What race?

LINCOLN: The human race!

Tall-man Stories

Was Lincoln born tall?

Well, he was always big for his age—and strong, too. By the time he was seventeen years old, Lincoln was "six feet four inches, nearly." He had to duck his head to go through a doorway.

Someone, noticing his long legs, said Abe Lincoln "looked as if he were made for wading in deep water."

Lincoln probably liked being tall. Whenever he met another tall man, Lincoln wanted to find out who was the taller.

Here are some tall-man stories and jokes.

Most of them are true stories about Lincoln.

Some are stories people made up.

Some are jokes that Lincoln liked to tell or listen to.

Muddy Feet

When Abe Lincoln was a boy, his stepmother liked to joke about how tall he was growing.

"Abe," she would say, "I don't care if your feet are dirty. I can scrub the floor. But you'd better wash your head, or you'll be rubbing dirt on my clean whitewashed ceiling."

One day his stepmother was away. And Abe saw some little boys wading in a mud puddle near the house. That gave Abe Lincoln an idea.

He picked the boys up one by one.

He carried them to the house.

He turned them upside down—and he walked their muddy feet across the ceiling!

Abe's stepmother came in.

She laughed at the foot tracks on the ceiling.

She laughed so hard she had to sit down.

"Abe!" she said. "You ought to be spanked!"

Then Abe painted the ceiling with fresh whitewash, and he made it look even cleaner than it did before.

How Long Should a Man's Legs Be?

When Lincoln was a lawyer, two friends came to him and said:

"Lincoln, we want you to settle an argument for us. Tell us, exactly how long should a man's legs be?"

Now one friend had very short legs.

The other friend had very long legs.

"Hmmmmm," Lincoln said. "I never gave this matter much thought. But now that I think of it, I would say——" Lincoln stopped.

He looked at the friend with short legs.

He looked at the friend with long legs.

"Well," Lincoln went on, "I would say *a man's legs should be exactly long enough to reach from his body to the ground.*"

The Longest Leg

One day a man came to Abraham Lincoln's law office. He saw Lincoln sitting with one leg stretched across the desk.

"Why Mr. Lincoln," said the man, "that's the longest leg I've ever seen!"

"Here's another just like it," said Lincoln. And he put his other leg across the desk.

A Man to Look Up to

In May, 1860, the Republican party nominated Lincoln to run for President. The next day, a group of men came to Lincoln's home in Springfield, Illinois. They came to give Lincoln official notice of his nomination.

One of the visitors was tall Judge Kelley from Pennsylvania.

The Judge looked at Lincoln.

Lincoln looked at the Judge.

"What's your height?" Lincoln asked.

"Six feet three inches," said the judge. "What's yours, Mr. Lincoln?"

"Six feet four inches," said Lincoln.

"Then," said the Judge, "Pennsylvania bows to Illinois. For years I have been wishing for a President I could look up to. I've found him at last!"

Here are two "tall" jokes from Joe Miller's joke book:

Out West there is a man so tall he has to climb a ladder to shave himself.

In Slickville, there is a 10-year-old boy who is so tall that his head does not know when his feet are cold.

A Tall Man With a Long Memory

A soldier who was going home to see his parents stopped at the White House to visit President Lincoln.

"I remember you," Lincoln said. "You're from Illinois. I stopped by your farm one day. That was about 25 years ago. I recollect that we stood talking out near the barnyard gate while I sharpened my jackknife on your whetstone."

"Yes," said the soldier. "You did. But where did you put that whetstone? We never could find it afterward. We figured maybe you took it with you."

"No, no!" said President Lincoln. "I put it on top of the gate post—that high one."

When the soldier got to his home in Illinois, the first thing he did was to look for the whetstone. He found it just where Lincoln said he put it—on top of the high gate post.

Short & Sweet

Tall Mr. Lincoln picked a short woman to be his wife. And he liked to joke about that sometimes.

A story told about the Lincolns went like this:

Soon after Lincoln was elected President, a crowd gathered under his windows to serenade him. Then they called for Lincoln to come out and talk to them.

Lincoln stepped onto the balcony with his wife. He wanted to make his greeting short and sweet. So he simply said, "Here I am and here is Mrs. Lincoln. That's the *long* and the *short* of it."

Absent-minded People

Once, before Lincoln was President, he made a speech in New York City.

It was an important speech. Lincoln spent a long time writing it. And he got dressed up for it. He wore a brand-new suit. But he forgot to take a long black pencil from behind his ear.

The pencil was there all through his speech.

When Lincoln became President, a friend reminded him about the speech and the pencil.

"Yes, I was absent-minded," said President Lincoln. "And that reminds me of the story about the absent-minded Englishman: When he went to bed he put his clothes into the bed and threw himself over the back of a chair."

Lincoln probably read about this absent-minded Englishman in his favorite joke book.

Here's another joke Lincoln could have told from Joe Miller's joke book:

There was the absent-minded Congressman who tried to smoke a spoon and stir his coffee with a cigar.

A Lincoln Riddle, Two Puns...

LINCOLN: If you call a sheep's tail a leg, how many legs will a sheep have?

MAN: Five legs, of course.

LINCOLN: Wrong. A sheep has four legs. Even if you call a tail a leg, it is still a tail.

Lincoln used this riddle to help him win an argument. Lincoln was trying to explain that just *saying* a thing is true does not make it true.

It is said that President Lincoln was walking up Pennsylvania Avenue with Mr. Seward, Secretary of State. Mr. Seward pointed to a sign with the name T. R. STRONG.

"Ha!" said Lincoln. "T R Strong, but coffee are stronger."

Some men were telling President Lincoln about their trip West. They told about a lake in Nebraska that had an Indian name. "I can't remember the Indian name," said one of the men. "But I know it means Weeping Water."

"Well," said Lincoln, "as Laughing Water is

Minne-haha, Weeping Water must be Minnie-boohoo."

...and a Joke

Lincoln read this one in Joe Miller's joke book:

Last winter, it is said, a cow floated down the Mississippi on a piece of ice. And she became so cold that since then she gives ice cream instead of milk.

And Another Riddle

Lincoln may have heard this riddle when he was a boy in Indiana. He used it when he was President to show that the right answer in arithmetic can sometimes be the wrong answer when you are dealing with pigeons or people:

LINCOLN: If there be three pigeons on the fence, and you fire and kill one, how many will there be left?

ANSWER: Two?

LINCOLN: No. There will be none left. For the other two birds, frightened by the shot, would have flown away.

Whose Boots?

Lincoln had always blacked his own boots (polished his own shoes) when he lived in Illinois. And when he became President and went to live in the White House, he didn't see any reason to change.

One morning Mr. Chase, the Secretary of the Treasury, came to the White House and found President Lincoln blacking his boots.

"Mr. Lincoln!" said Chase. "Gentlemen don't black their own boots in Washington!"

Without even looking up from his work, Lincoln asked, "Then whose boots *do* they black?"

The Town of Lincoln

Lincoln was a modest man. When someone asked if the town of Lincoln was named after him, Lincoln replied, "Well, it was named *after* I was, if that is what you mean."

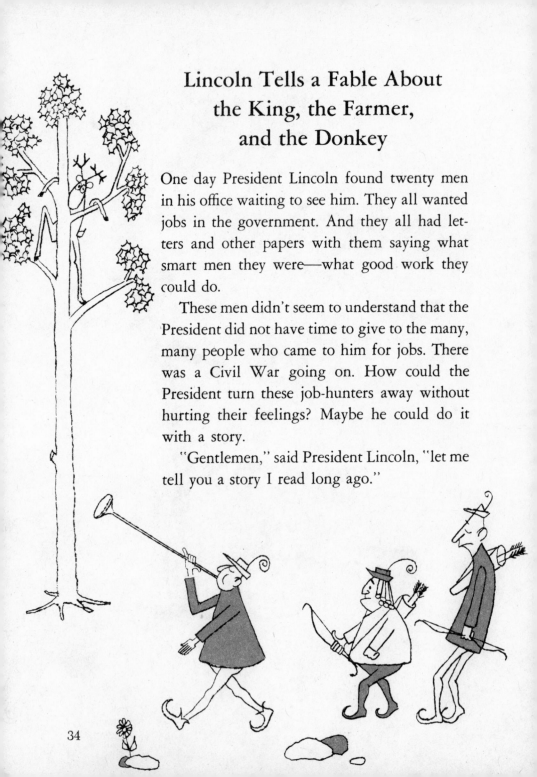

Lincoln Tells a Fable About the King, the Farmer, and the Donkey

One day President Lincoln found twenty men in his office waiting to see him. They all wanted jobs in the government. And they all had letters and other papers with them saying what smart men they were—what good work they could do.

These men didn't seem to understand that the President did not have time to give to the many, many people who came to him for jobs. There was a Civil War going on. How could the President turn these job-hunters away without hurting their feelings? Maybe he could do it with a story.

"Gentlemen," said President Lincoln, "let me tell you a story I read long ago."

There was once a King who wanted to go hunting. He called the man who was Chief Weatherman and Court Minister.

"Tell me," said the King, "will it rain to-day?"

"No, your Majesty," said the Chief Weatherman and Court Minister. "The weather is clear. It won't rain. Good hunting to you!"

The King set out with his hunting party. On the way they met a farmer riding on a donkey. "Don't try to go hunting today, Your Majesty," said the farmer. "It is going to rain."

The King laughed and rode on. Surely the Court Minister knew better than a simple farmer!

But just as the King reached the forest, it began to rain. Oh, how it poured! The King and everyone with him were soaked to the skin.

When the King got home, he fired the Court Minister. Then he sent for the farmer.

"From now on," said the King, "you will have the job of Chief Weatherman and Court Minister. Now tell me, how did you know it would rain?"

"I didn't," said the farmer. "It's my donkey who knows when it is going to rain. He puts his ears forward when wet weather is coming; he puts them back when it's going to be dry. So you see, Your Majesty, I cannot take the job."

The King sent the farmer away and sent for the donkey. And the King gave the donkey the job of Chief Weatherman and Court Minister.

"And that," said Lincoln, "is when the King made a great mistake."

"Why do you say that?" asked one of the job-hunters.

"Why, ever since that time," said Lincoln, "every donkey wants a job with the government."

The men couldn't help laughing. And then Lincoln told them, "Gentlemen, leave your letters and papers with me, and when the war is over, you will hear from me."

Funnyman Artemus Ward

A young man called Artemus Ward was a famous American comic when Lincoln was President. Lincoln liked the young man's stories and jokes so much that he invited Ward to visit the White House.

Here are some of the things Artemus Ward said and did that made President Lincoln laugh.

A Riddle

Artemus Ward made up this riddle for Tad Lincoln, the President's son:

WARD: Why was Goliath surprised when David hit him with a stone?

TAD: Why?

WARD: Because such a thing had never entered his head before.

As Big a Liar

Lincoln liked to tell about the time Artemus Ward was invited to a party.

Mr. Ward was wearing his old country clothes. But he wanted to show that he felt at home, so he stepped right up to a very proud-looking lady and said, "Jeepers creepers! You sure are handsome!"

The woman was angry. "I wish I could say the same thing about you," she said.

"You could, Madam," answered Artemus Ward, "if you were as big a liar as I am."

Scary Scarecrow

Artemus Ward was bragging about his father.

"My father was a great artist," he said. "Everything my father made was true to life. Once he made a scarecrow. And gentlemen that scarecrow was so scary the crows brought back the corn they had stolen two years before."

Big Feet

Artemus Ward knew the joke people told about Lincoln's big feet. It went like this:

It was winter and Lincoln and a friend were walking along an icy road. "Brrr!" Lincoln complained about the cold.

His companion looked down at Lincoln's feet. "No wonder you are so cold," said the friend. "There is so much of you on the ground."

Bigger Feet

"Mr. Lincoln," said Ward, "maybe you think you have big feet. But my wife's feet are so big that her toes come around the corner two minutes before she comes along!"

McClellan Has the Slows

At the beginning of the Civil War George B. McClellan was General in Chief of the Northern army.

And General McClellan was one of President Lincoln's biggest problems.

McClellan would not move the Northern army out of training camp.

If only he would march south with his men, McClellan could fight and win some battles. And then, thought Lincoln, maybe the war would be over quickly.

But instead of marching south, McClellan stayed in camp and made excuses:

He said his horses were tired.

He said he needed more men.

He said he needed more supplies.

McClellan had many more men, more horses,

more supplies than the generals of the South. But still he didn't move out of camp.

"McClellan has the slows," said President Lincoln. And for months Lincoln tried to be patient.

Sometimes he would blow off steam by making jokes or telling stories.

Here are some of Lincoln's jokes and funny sayings about General McClellan.

Borrow the Army

"If General McClellan does not want to use the army," said Lincoln, "I would like to borrow it —provided it can be made to do something."

A Pass to Richmond

President Lincoln had been trying for a long time to get McClellan to march south with his army and take the city of Richmond, Virginia.

One day, while Lincoln was worrying about this problem, a business man came to see him. The man asked for a pass so that he could go to—of all places—Richmond, Virginia.

"A pass to Richmond?" said Lincoln with a sigh. "My dear sir, it would do you no good. I have given McClellan passes for two hundred and fifty thousand men . . . and not one of them has got there yet!"

Sleep Standing Up

Lincoln said to a friend, "If I gave General McClellan all the men he asks for, they would have to sleep standing up."

"Why would they have to sleep standing up?" the friend wanted to know.

"Because," said Lincoln, "there would be so many men there wouldn't be enough room for them to lie down."

Tired Horses

General McClellan sent President Lincoln a message saying he needed fresh horses. All his horses were tired—"sore-tongued and *fatigued*," McClellan wrote.

President Lincoln sent a sharp reply to the General:

"Will you pardon me for asking what the horses of your army have done . . . that *fatigues* anything?"

Have Captured Two Cows

Everyone knew that President Lincoln was having a hard time with General George B. Mc-Clellan. There were many stories and jokes about the President and the General. This is one of the stories that got around:

"I *must* have more information about what your army is doing," wrote Lincoln to General McClellan.

So McClellan sent Lincoln a telegram:
HAVE CAPTURED TWO COWS. WHAT SHALL I DO WITH THEM?

Lincoln sent a quick telegram in reply: MILK 'EM, GEORGE.

"I Will Get Off"

The Governor of Massachusetts told about the time President Lincoln showed him a long letter from General McClellan. The Governor could not help smiling when he read it. McClellan was not doing very well as a general. But his long letter to Lincoln was full of advice on how to run the country.

"What are you going to say in answer to the letter?" asked the Governor.

"Nothing," said Lincoln. "But it makes me think of the man whose horse kicked up and stuck his foot through the stirrup. The man said to the horse, 'If you are going to get on, I will get off.'"

A Wish

Lincoln was walking down the dark, dimly lit stairway in the War Department building.

A young officer, carrying important papers for the Secretary of War, was rushing up the same stairway. He crashed head-on into the President.

"Ten thousand pardons!" the officer gasped.

"One is enough," said President Lincoln. "I wish the whole army could charge like that."

Lost

The way a certain General was wandering around in the South "as if he were lost," said Lincoln, reminded him of this story:

A man in Illinois went with some friends to visit the state jail. It was a big place, and the man got separated from his friends and couldn't find his way out.

He wandered up and down the corridors and at last he saw a prisoner looking through the bars of his cell.

The man called to the prisoner: "Hey! How do you get out of this place?"

"If I knew that, I wouldn't be here," the prisoner yelled back.

Famous Liars

In Lincoln's time there were a number of popular stories about famous liars. Or about people who had a way of stretching the truth to make a tall story.

Sometimes the way army generals stretched the truth reminded Lincoln of these stories. Here are a couple of them.

Tall and Narrow

Once there was a man who always exaggerated. He tried to break this habit, but nothing would work.

At last he had a plan. He told his servant: "The next time you hear me telling *too* big a lie, just step on my toe. That will remind me to stop exaggerating."

That same evening, the man was telling friends about his trip to Europe. He began to tell about a building he saw there.

"It was a mile *long* and half a mile *high*," said the man.

"My!" said one of his friends. "And how *wide* was that building?"

But just then the man felt his toe being stepped on. He realized he had been stretching things a bit. So to make up for it, he said, "How wide? Ohhhh, only about twelve inches."

Arithmetic

For a minute, a visitor to the White House thought Lincoln himself was stretching the facts.

The visitor had asked Lincoln how many soldiers were in the Southern army.

"Twelve hundred thousand," said the President slowly. "That is to say, one million, two hundred thousand."

"Good heavens!" the visitor cried. "Impossible!"

"No doubt of it," said Lincoln. "You see, when our generals lose a battle, they always say the enemy had at least three times as many men as we did. Now, we have 400,000 men in the field. And 3 times 4 makes 12. Don't you see it?"

$$400,000 \times 3 = 1,200,000$$

Leg Cases

During the Civil War young soldiers sometimes became so frightened they would run away in the middle of a battle.

President Lincoln felt sorry for these young men, and he would often pardon them when they were arrested for running away.

He called them *leg cases.*

"Why do you call them *leg cases?*" someone asked.

"Well," said Lincoln, "they remind me of the

story about the Irish soldier who always boasted about how brave he was. But the minute a battle began, he would run away. His captain asked him why he ran away if he was so brave.

" 'Captain,' said the soldier, 'my heart is as brave as the heart of any hero. But somehow, when danger comes near, my cowardly legs run away with me.' "

A Big Hog

It was just after the Battle of Bull Run during the Civil War. The battlefield was full of dead and dying soldiers.

A curiosity-seeker asked for a pass to the battlefield so that he could "see the sights."

"I don't think you would really want to see those terrible sights," Lincoln told the man.

Then, because the man looked so disappointed, Lincoln tried to send him away smiling.

"That reminds me of a story my old father once told me," Lincoln said, "about a farmer in Cortland County who raised a hog.

"The hog was so big that people came from miles around to see it. A stranger heard the farmer boasting about the enormous hog, and asked if he could see it.

" 'Sure,' said the farmer. 'But you will have to pay a quarter to look at him.'

"The stranger took a long hard look at the farmer. Then he pulled a quarter out of his pocket, handed it over, and walked away.

" 'Hey!' said the farmer. 'Don't you want to see the hog?'

" 'No thanks,' the stranger replied. 'I've seen as big a hog as I want to see.' "

Lincoln's Looks

Lincoln often joked about his looks. So did other people. Lincoln was tall—"six feet four inches, nearly," as he put it. And he was thin. This made him look even taller. His hands were big. So were his feet. So was his nose. He had a habit of running his hands through his black hair so that sometimes it stuck out every which way.

One visitor to the White House wrote his wife that Lincoln was "a very honest and kindly man." And in the same letter he said:

"The President is, I think, the ugliest man I ever saw."

Another visitor said Lincoln was the handsomest man she had ever seen.

How could the same man look ugly and handsome?

Many people came to see Lincoln and then wrote about what he looked like. And many, many people agreed about one thing:

When Lincoln smiled, his whole face changed. It seemed to light up and become beautiful.

How to Win a Pocketknife

Lincoln said this happened to him when he was a traveling lawyer:

A stranger came up to Lincoln and said, "Excuse me, sir. I have something that belongs to you."

"What do you mean?" Lincoln asked the stranger.

The stranger took a jackknife out of his pocket. "Many years ago," he said, "someone gave me this jackknife. He told me that when I found a man uglier than myself I must hand the knife over to him. Allow me to say, sir, that I think the knife now belongs to you."

Something in It

John Ericsson wrote to President Lincoln about a warship he had invented. It was completely covered with *steel.*

This was a new idea. Many experts said it would not work. Mr. Ericsson came to a meeting to explain his idea.

Three top Navy officers were at the meeting. President Lincoln himself was there. And so were the members of his Cabinet.

Mr. Ericsson showed them a cardboard model of the ship he wanted to build. He named his ship the *Monitor.* The *Monitor* would be small, he said. It could move fast. It would be able to go in shallow water. It would have a gun turret that could turn 'round and 'round.

Some of the men said it would never work.

Some of them even made fun of it. "It looks like a cheese box on a raft," said one man.

But President Lincoln had the last word. He held the cardboard model of the *Monitor* in his hand and told the men, "All I have to say is what the girl said when she put her foot in the stocking. It strikes me there is something in it."

And it turned out that Lincoln was right. Ericsson built the *Monitor*. And very soon, in the famous battle with the big Southern ship, the *Merrimac*, the little *Monitor* proved her worth.

People agreed that if it were not for President Lincoln, Ericsson would not have been given a chance to build the *Monitor*.

How to Get Rid of a Pest

Judge Carter, a friend of President Lincoln, came to the White House one day and found the President laughing so hard he could hardly talk.

At last Lincoln stopped laughing and explained to Judge Carter how he had just got rid of a man who had been pestering him for weeks.

Every week this man used to come up from Philadelphia to give Lincoln advice on what laws to pass, how to run the war, which people should have jobs in the government, and so on and so on.

The man from Philadelphia had just been in to see Lincoln again. And he had talked on and on and on. At last Lincoln lost his patience. He decided he had to get rid of this pest once and for all—even if it meant being rude.

Lincoln went over to a cupboard in the corner of the room. He opened the door and took a bottle from the shelf.

Then Lincoln looked very hard at the man from Philadelphia—especially at his bald head.

"Did you ever try this stuff for your hair?" asked Lincoln, holding up the bottle.

"No, sir, I never did," his visitor replied.

"Well then," said Lincoln, "I advise you to try it. I will give you this bottle. If at first you don't succeed, try, try again. Keep it up. They say it will make hair grow on a pumpkin.

"Now take this bottle and come back in eight or ten months and tell me how it works."

And Lincoln shoved the bottle into the hand of the very surprised man from Philadelphia, led him to the door, and out of the room.

"I Didn't Want to Hurt You"

At a meeting of his Cabinet, President Lincoln read an important message he had written about slavery. Lincoln asked if anyone had any suggestion—any word he thought should be changed.

Mr. Seward, Secretary of State, suggested that a word be added to one sentence. Lincoln agreed. About ten minutes later, Mr. Seward suggested another change. Lincoln agreed to Seward's second change, too.

"But why didn't you suggest both of your changes at once?" asked Lincoln. And Lincoln said Mr. Seward reminded him of the hired man in Illinois who was driving a team of oxen:

The hired man, said Lincoln, came running to the farmer with bad news: One ox had dropped dead.

The farmer was sorry to hear it.

The hired man stood around and waited a while. At last he told the farmer, "The other ox died too."

"Why didn't you tell me in the first place that both oxen were dead?" asked the farmer.

"I didn't want to hurt you by telling you too much at one time," replied the hired man.

Wolf Dog

Lincoln had a general who bragged a lot but wasn't so good at fighting. When Lincoln heard that the general had run away from the enemy, he may have been reminded of the story about the man and his new hunting dog:

"That new dog of mine is a great fighter," the hunter bragged. "Just show him a pack of wolves and he'll go after them and eat 'em up."

And the man sent his dog into the underbrush to scare up some wolves.

Wolves and dog went racing across the fields. The hunter followed far behind. When he reached a farm yard, he asked the farmer, "Have you seen a wolf dog and a pack of wolves?"

"Yep," said the farmer.

"How were they going?"

"Pretty fast."

"What was their position when you saw them?"

"Well," said the farmer slowly, "the dog was a leetle bit ahead."

Important Business

An angry farmer came up to President Lincoln at a White House gathering. "Some soldiers helped themselves to my hay and my horse, Mr. President," said the farmer. "And I want you to see to it that I get my horse back right away."

Now President Lincoln was busy day and night. He had many important questions to think about. So he explained to the farmer as patiently as he could:

"Why, my dear sir, if I tried to take care of every person's business, I would have work enough for twenty presidents!"

After the farmer left, Lincoln turned to a friend and said, "That farmer reminds me of something that happened to Jack Chase, a riverboat captain I used to know in Illinois.

"It was quite a trick to take the boat over the rapids in the river, and Captain Jack always took the wheel himself to steer the boat through them.

"One day the rapids were especially rough and Captain Jack was working hard to get the boat through.

"Suddenly a boy came up and pulled at Jack's

coattail. 'Say, Mr. Captain,' said the boy, 'stop the boat a minute! I've lost my apple overboard.' "

Lincoln Gives a Book Review

A well-known man read aloud to President Lincoln some chapters from a book he was writing.

"Tell me, Mr. Lincoln," said the man, "what do you think of my book?"

Lincoln didn't think much of it. But he didn't want to hurt the author's feelings, so he said:

"Well, for those who like that sort of thing, I think it is just about the sort of thing they would like."

The Next President

And when someone asked Lincoln who would be the next President, he is supposed to have answered:

"I cannot say for certain who will be the people's choice for President. But to the best of my belief, it will be the successful candidate."

Help!

The Northern states and the Southern states had been fighting for about two years. An officer came to President Lincoln with bad news.

The officer could see that President Lincoln was very, very tired and very, very sad.

"I wish I were bringing you better news, sir," said the officer. "Or at least I wish I were bringing you information that would help you conquer or get rid of those rebel states."

Now Lincoln felt that his most important job was to keep all the states in the Union. He did not want to let any of them go.

To make his point, and to cheer up the officer, Lincoln said, "That reminds me of a story . . ."

Some hunters were surprised by a bear that suddenly came into their camp. All but one of the men climbed trees or hid behind rocks. One man crept up behind the bear, grabbed it by the ears, and held on for dear life.

The bear ran 'round and 'round. The man began hollering for help.

"Why do you need help?" called his friends. "You're hanging on all right."

"I want you to help me let this bear go!" shouted the man.

"Now," said Lincoln, "If I could only let the rebel states go, I would have no problem. But I must hold on to them and keep them in the Union."

Big Stink

Some men came to Lincoln and told him, "You got rid of your Secretary of War, and you found a better man to put in his place. Why don't you get rid of *all* your old advisors in the same way?"

Lincoln told these men they reminded him of a story . . .

A farmer in Illinois had trouble with skunks. The skunks were stealing his chickens at night.

The farmer's wife kept after him to get rid of those skunks. So one moonlit night the farmer went out with his shotgun while his wife waited in the house.

The farmer's wife heard a shot ring out, and soon the farmer came back.

"Any luck?" his wife asked.

"Well," said the farmer, "I hid behind the woodpile near the chicken house. And pretty soon I saw a skunk—and another and another. Seven skunks in all. I took aim and shot one skunk. Killed him dead."

"But what about the other skunks?" cried the wife. "Why didn't you get rid of *all* the skunks?"

"Well," said the farmer as he put his gun away, "the first skunk made such a big stink, I decided to leave the other six skunks alone."

"It Doesn't Hurt Me..."

A newspaper editor printed many lies about President Lincoln.

"Why do you let him print such things?" asked Lincoln's friends. "Why don't you stop him?"

"Oh, I don't really mind," said Lincoln. "It reminds me of the big fellow who let his little wife hit him over the head with a stick. He told his friends, 'Let her alone. It doesn't hurt me, and it does her a power of good.'"

Doctor's Orders

Most of the joke-book writers in President Lincoln's time wanted people to think that all their jokes and stories came from Lincoln himself.

A joke in one of these books pretends to tell of the time Lincoln spoke to a soldier who was in jail:

Lincoln asked the soldier why he was in jail. "Because I followed the doctor's orders," said the soldier.

"What do you mean?" asked Lincoln.

The soldier explained:

"One morning I did not feel very well, so I went to see the doctor. He was busy writing and when I came in he just looked up at me and said, 'Well, you do look sick. You had better take something.'

"He then went on writing and left me standing behind him. I looked around and I did not see anything I could take—except his watch. So I took that. And that's why I'm here."

A Bad Example

President Lincoln told the story of a governor who visited the state prison.

The governor talked to the prisoners and asked what crimes they had committed. Each prisoner said he had never done anything wrong. To hear them talk, you would have thought they were all innocent, good men.

At last the governor came to one prisoner who said, "I am a thief and I deserve to be in jail."

"Then I must pardon you," said the governor, "and get you out of this place. You seem to be the only criminal in this prison, and I don't want you here setting a bad example to all these good men I have been talking to."

At the Theater

Some joke-book writers pretended that the man in this story was President Lincoln:

It is time for the play to begin.

The theater is almost dark.

A man hurries in and sits down.

He puts his high silk hat, open side up, on the seat next to him. He does not see that a fat woman is about to sit there.

CRUNCH! The fat woman sits on the hat.

She jumps up.

The man picks up his hat—what is left of it.

He looks at it sadly. Then he looks at the woman.

"Madam," he says, "I could have told you my hat would not fit *before* you tried it on."

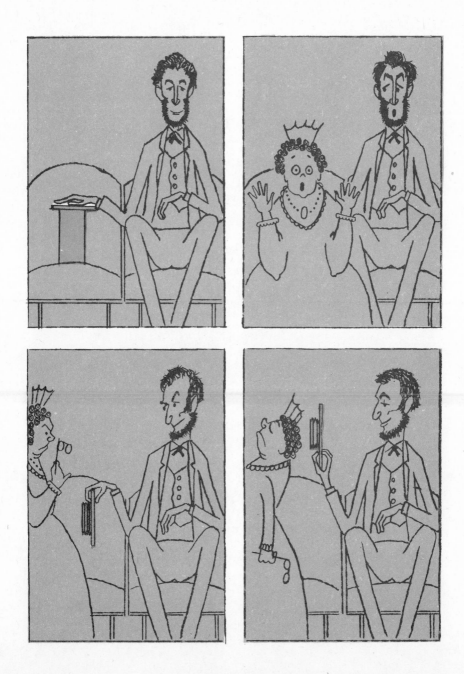

Lincoln's Favorite Joke

And here is the joke about himself that Lincoln liked best of all. He said it was the best story about himself he had ever read in the papers:

Two Quaker women were talking about who would win the war—President Lincoln for the United States, or Jefferson Davis, who was President of the Southern rebel states.

FIRST QUAKER WOMAN: I think Jefferson Davis will win.

SECOND QUAKER WOMAN: Why does thee think so?

FIRST QUAKER WOMAN: Because he is a praying man.

SECOND QUAKER WOMAN: Abraham Lincoln is a praying man too.

FIRST QUAKER WOMAN: Yes, but the Lord will think Abraham is joking.

About Lincoln and Jokes

Young Abe Lincoln read everything he could get hold of. And he seemed never to forget anything he read.

Young Abe Lincoln listened to everything that went on around him. And he seemed never to forget anything he heard.

Lincoln's memory was like a grab-bag full of treasures. All through his life he could reach in and pull out a treasure—just the right fact or story or anecdote he needed

——to prove a point

——or help him answer a question

——or cheer up the people around him.

"You speak of Lincoln stories," President Lincoln once said. "I don't think that is . . . correct. . . ." And Lincoln explained that he almost never *invented* stories. He told stories and jokes he remembered hearing or reading.

Lincoln told a friend that he got in the habit of telling stories and jokes when he was very young. He had often found that telling a funny story was a good way to explain something serious. "I am not simply a story-teller," said Lincoln. "It is not the story itself, but its *purpose* that interests me."

Then Lincoln went on to say that, as President, he had to say *no* to many people who asked for special favors. And sometimes he had to tell people they were doing things they should not be doing. Or he had to tell someone to do something that was hard to do.

A joke could make a *no* or a scolding or an order easier to take.

Sometimes a visitor asked President Lincoln questions. And Lincoln could not answer, because the answer was a secret. Then Lincoln would tell a story and make the visitor forget his questions.

President Lincoln often kept a joke book or a book of humorous stories in his desk drawer. Some people asked, "Why does the President waste his time on jokes?"

But many people understood that Lincoln needed something to make him laugh. About a month after he became President, the Civil War began. President Lincoln had big problems and heavy responsibilities. Sometimes it seemed to him that he would break down under the strain. If he could smile or laugh—just for a moment—he could manage to keep going.

Lincoln himself said, "I laugh because I must not cry."

"Lincoln had the saddest face I ever tried to paint," said Francis Carpenter, an artist.

Mr. Carpenter lived in the White House while he was painting President Lincoln's portrait. And Carpenter noticed that when the President felt saddest he would try to get relief by telling a joke or reading a book of humorous stories.

Lincoln believed that jokes are good for children, too. He thought jokes and riddles were good fun and helped sharpen the wits.

Lincoln agreed with a friend who said it was as important to teach jokes and riddles in school as it was to teach reading and writing and arithmetic.

Maybe you will want to tell some of these Lincoln jokes sometimes

———to prove a point

———to answer a question

———or just for fun.

Some Important Dates in Lincoln's Life

1809
February 12
A boy baby is born in a log cabin in Kentucky. He is named Abraham, after his grandfather.

1816
Abe Lincoln is almost 8 years old when the Lincoln family moves to Little Pigeon Creek in Indiana.

1818
Lincoln's mother dies. Abe is only 9 years old, and his sister Sarah is 11.

1819
Lincoln's father goes to Kentucky and comes back with a wife. Now Abe and his sister have a kind and loving stepmother to take care of them. And they have a stepbrother and stepsisters to play with.

1820-1830

Abe Lincoln chops down trees in the forests of Indiana and splits rails to make fences. He plows the fields, plants them, shucks corn, builds pigpens, butchers hogs, milks cows. He wrestles, cracks jokes, tells stories, and reads, reads, reads every book he can lay his hands on. When Abe is 19 years old, he builds a flatboat and takes a load of farm produce down the Mississippi River to New Orleans.

1830

The Lincolns move to a new farm in Illinois.

1831

Lincoln, now 22 years old, says good-bye to his family and goes to New Salem, Illinois. He gets a job as a store clerk.

1832

Lincoln enlists as a soldier in the Black Hawk war. The other volunteers in his company elect him Captain.

1833

Lincoln is Postmaster in New Salem. He learns how to measure land and becomes a surveyor. He also begins to study law.

1834

Lincoln, at the age of 25, is elected to the Illinois legislature.

1836

Lincoln gets a license to be a lawyer. He is elected to the Illinois legislature for the second time.

1837

Lincoln moves to Springfield, Illinois, where he will live and be a lawyer for many years.

1838-1842

Lincoln is elected to the Illinois legislature again in 1838 and in 1840. When he does not have to be in the legislature, he keeps busy as a traveling lawyer.

1842

Lincoln marries Mary Todd. He is 33 years old.

1847

Lincoln, who has been elected to Congress, goes to Washington, D.C., with his wife and two children.

1849-1860

The Lincolns come back to Springfield, Illinois. Lincoln is a traveling lawyer again.

1860

The Republican party nominates Abraham Lincoln for President. Lincoln wins the election.

1861
March 4
Lincoln is inaugurated as the sixteenth President of the United States. He is 52 years old.

April 12
Fort Sumter is fired on. The Civil War begins.

1864
Lincoln is elected for his second term as President.

1865
April 9
General Lee surrenders to General Grant, and the Civil War is over.

April 14
President Lincoln is shot.

April 15
The President dies. "Now he belongs to the ages."